SO-CEX-406

How to play the

Harmonica

IAN KEAREY

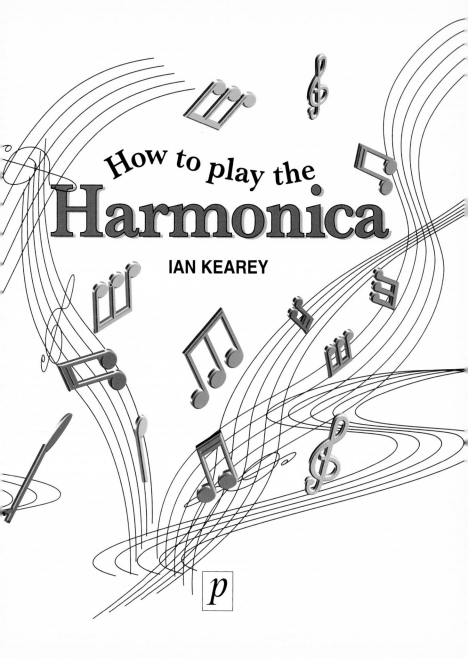

How to play the
Harmonica

IAN KEAREY

p

This is a Parragon Publishing Book
This edition published in 2000

Parragon Publishing
Queen Street House
4 Queen Street
Bath BA1 1HE, UK

ISBN 0-75254-262-1

Produced by Haldane Mason, London

Printed in China

Contents

Introduction

When you hear a harmonica being played, what images and sounds does it conjure up? The jaunty rhythms of a folk dance, or the long, high notes of a steam-train whistle? The melancholy, plaintive counterpoint to a country song, or the marching steps of a First World War tune? The raw intensity of the blues, or the complex virtuosity of jazz? The funkiness of a Stevie Wonder, or the apparent simplicity of a Woody Guthrie or Bob Dylan? The list could be almost endless and the amazing thing is, that this extraordinary variety of sound and emotion is created by a very ordinary-looking and inexpensive mass-produced instrument.

Since its invention over 150 years ago, the harmonica has truly laid claim to be the 'people's instrument'; millions have been manufactured and sold on every continent, and have been used to play in a bewildering variety of musical styles. This popularity is due, in part, to its simplicity of design: you can carry it anywhere, it doesn't need to be tuned and if it gets damaged or doesn't work, a new one is cheaply bought. But the real secret of the harmonica's success is that it is so easy to pick up and make a pleasant noise through – all you have to do at the beginning is breathe into it. Give even very small children a harmonica, and the random chords and notes they produce already sound like a half-formed tune; and once you understand how the instrument works and how to get the best out of it, you'll be able to extend your creative and interpretive talents greatly.

That said, you have to work at it – competence doesn't come immediately, and that's where this book comes in. But the harmonica is possibly the friendliest of all instruments for a beginner to learn, and the satisfaction of being able to play what you want, when and where you want, will quickly repay the study and practice you put in. Above all, enjoy playing the harmonica and going through the learning process – once you get started, it's hard to put it down!

Stevie Wonder started learning the harmonica when very young, and became a child prodigy.

How to use this book

The techniques of playing and tunes featured in the following pages are based around a three-octave, 12-hole diatonic harmonica tuned to the key of C, although they can be easily adapted to smaller harmonicas in the same key. The aim of the book is to provide the complete beginner, with no musical training or knowledge, with a simple guide to playing melodies and accompaniments to well-known songs and tunes; from there, more advanced and complex techniques are introduced, as well as an introduction to playing both 'crossed' and 'straight' blues harmonica.

When you first start playing the harmonica, you may be surprised at how quickly you can play simple tunes without needing to read them from standard musical notation; in addition, many famous harmonica players have never learned to read music and 'play by ear'. However, not everyone has the facility to pick up a tune from hearing it, and a basic knowledge of reading music is invaluable in the long run, so persevere with the information given in Chapter 2 and it will pay dividends in expanding your repertoire.

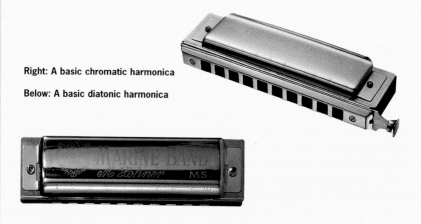

Right: A basic chromatic harmonica

Below: A basic diatonic harmonica

Because harmonicas are played by exhaling and inhaling, a particular system of notation for harmonicas has been developed and is widely used. In this, each of the 12 mouth holes is given a number, 1 standing for the left-hand hole that produces the lowest notes, and 12 for the right-hand hole that makes the highest notes. These numbers are not always printed or embossed on the instrument, but you will find that a little practice enables you to find them easily.

Lowest note   **Highest note**

1   2   3   4   5   6   7   8   9   10   11   12

The notes produced by blowing, or exhaling, are given as plain numbers:

    1   2   3   2   3   4   4   5   6

The notes produced by drawing, or inhaling, as given as numbers within circles:

   ① ② ③   ② ③ ④   ⑤ ⑥ ⑦

Right: This chromatic harmonica is an example of how designs can vary.

Chapter **1**

About the harmonica

'har•mon•i•ca n a small rectangular wind instrument with free reeds recessed in air slots from which tones are sounded by exhaling and inhaling'

Merriam-Webster's Collegiate Dictionary, 10th ed., 1995

Larry Adler is probably the most famous harmonica player today, with a complete mastery of the chromatic harmonica.

A brief history

The name 'harmonica' was given to all sorts of strange and now obsolete instruments, ranging from musical glasses, through glass dulcimers to nails played with a bow, before it became synonymous with the term 'mouth-organ'. The instrument we know as the harmonica was first marketed by Charles Wheatstone (who also invented the concertina and the electric telegraph) in 1829, under the name of 'The Aeolina'. This high-flown name was soon dropped, and the inexpensive little instrument that was so easy to learn was taken up by all classes of people around the world.

All harmonicas at this time were diatonic (see page 16), which meant that it was not possible to play full chromatic tunes; this led to the harmonica becoming associated solely with popular and folk tunes until the 1920s, when chromatic harmonicas were first marketed. The ease with which the basic steps could be mastered led to harmonica bands and harmonica classes in schools; during the First World War, special funds were set up in both Britain and Germany to supply free harmonicas to all servicemen who applied, and the image of the cowboy playing his harmonica at the end of a long day is universally recognized.

In spite of this popularity, the musical establishment looked down on the harmonica: the *Oxford Companion to Music* of 1938 grudgingly approved of its use in schools because of the 'expectation that a proportion of children thus introduced to instrumental performance may be led to proceed to some instrument of more definite artistic possibilities.' However, the public around the world disagreed – in 1929, the manufacturers Hohner claimed to have produced over 30,000,000 instruments – and the introduction of the chromatic harmonica, quickly exploited to its full by virtuoso players such as Larry Adler, Tommy Reilly and Max Geldray, brought the harmonica to a prime place in the worlds of jazz and light classical music.

The folk and blues revival of the late 1950s and early 1960s propelled the harmonica back into the mainstream of popular music as Bob Dylan, the Beatles and the Rolling Stones matched its folk, country and blues qualities with rock 'n' roll and rhythm and blues to enjoy worldwide fame. Today, nearly all harmonicas are made in Germany, the USA and China, and the range of models runs into the hundreds, from inexpensive diatonic and novelty miniature harmonicas to four-octave chromatic and bass ones.

This enormous novelty harmonica was made in the 1930s.

How it works

The diatonic harmonica is the smallest and simplest of the 'free reed' instruments, which include the concertina, accordian, melodeon, harmonium or American organ, and Chinese sheng. In these instruments, each reed – a brass strip attached at one end to a brass frame or base – vibrates freely when air is moved from the unattached end to the other; the harmonica is the only one in which this process is controlled and directed solely by the mouth (all the others have buttons or keys). The mouthpiece assembly can be made of wood or plastic, and the casing on which the lips rest is usually metal.

Each hole of a diatonic harmonica mouthpiece is a 'tunnel' to two free reeds, placed at the top and bottom of the tunnel. The top reed, with the unattached end near the mouth hole, vibrates when it is blown, and the bottom reed, with the unattached end away from the mouth hole, when it is sucked, or drawn. Each mouth hole thus produces two notes, which are tuned to be next to each other on the scale.

Diatonic harmonica – top reeds

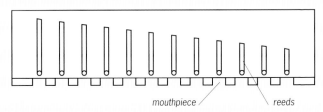

mouthpiece   *reeds*

Diatonic harmonica – bottom reeds

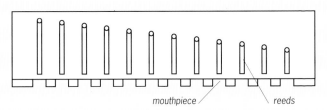

mouthpiece   *reeds*

Diatonic harmonicas are produced in a range of keys: C, D, E, F, G, A and Bb. A 12-hole harmonica in the key of C has a range of three octaves, starting and ending on C. The notes are equivalent to the white keys on a piano keyboard, with the lowest harmonica C being middle C on a piano.

Notes on 3-octave C harmonica

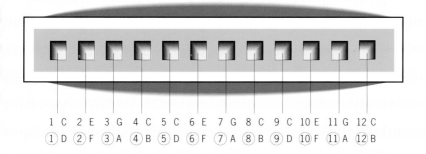

```
1 C   2 E   3 G   4 C   5 C   6 E   7 G   8 C   9 C   10 E  11 G  12 C
① D   ② F   ③ A   ④ B   ⑤ D   ⑥ F   ⑦ A   ⑧ B   ⑨ D   ⑩ F   ⑪ A   ⑫ B
```

Note that both 4 and 5 play the same note when blown, as do 8 and 9. This is to regularize the system, so that both octaves are played identicallly.

Right: A chromatic harmonica, as well as playing the 'natural' notes, plays the 'accidentals', or flats and sharps.

The harmonica family

The two basic types of harmonica are diatonic, as shown on pages 14 and 15, and chromatic, although there are variations on both of these. A diatonic harmonica in C plays the notes of a scale without the accidentals – sharps and flats (the black notes on a piano). Diatonic harmonicas in other keys are played in exactly the same way, but the musical notation is different (see Chapter 2). The most common variation on a diatonic harmonica, apart from the range of notes and size, is for the top and bottom reeds to be separated by a piece of wood or plastic, thus creating two tunnels, which allows for greater accuracy when playing single notes.

Take time to choose the right diatonic for you.

A chromatic harmonica in C produces all the notes of the scale, including the accidentals or black notes on a keyboard. Here, two sets of diatonic reeds are incorporated, one tuned to C and one to C#. There is a lever on the right of the mouthpiece: when this is pushed in, a bar is slid across the mouth holes that play the C reeds, so that only the C# reeds can be played. When the lever is retracted or left alone, the bar covers the C# reeds. Pushing and releasing the lever quickly allows you to play fully chromatic scales and tunes.

This extended range of notes means that the chromatic harmonica is the best choice for playing music that requires a full chromatic range, such as jazz or classical. It also means that chromatic harmonicas are a good deal heavier and more expensive than diatonic ones and that it takes longer to learn to use them to their full extent.

Despite variations, all chromatic harmonicas work the same way.

Looking after your harmonica

Talk to any number of harmonica players about how they look after and break in their instruments, and each one will come out with different advice, to the point of completely disagreeing with one another. Players' habits range from wrapping the harmonica in fine silk cloth or chamois leather to soaking it in water, beer, vodka or whisky! While these particular methods may work well for the individual, there are some basic ground rules that will ensure that your harmonica stays in good playing condition for a long time. Even with the best care, it won't last forever when played regularly, so don't persevere with a damaged or worn-out harmonica, because you won't be able to get the results you want and may become discouraged.

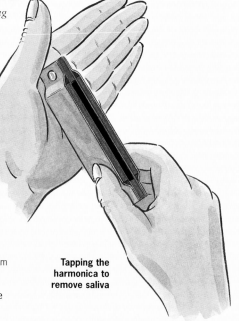

The most important thing is to keep your harmonica clean. As with all instruments that are blown, quite a lot of saliva and tiny particles from the mouth enter the harmonica while you play it; these can jam up the reeds and prevent them from vibrating, and in some cases they can be dislodged and fly into your mouth if you

Tapping the harmonica to remove saliva

draw hard. For this reason, it is a good idea to always rinse out your mouth thoroughly before playing.

To prevent a build-up of saliva, hold the harmonica by one end and tap the mouthpiece hard into the palm of your other hand, then take the other end and repeat the process. This should be done regularly, every few minutes or so, and always when you have finished playing.

Harmonicas are also damaged by dirt getting into the reeds, so keep your instrument in its box or case when you are not playing it, and don't be tempted to carry it around loose in a pocket or bag, however clean it may appear to be. To polish the casing, use a clean, soft, lint-free cloth.

If a crust builds up on the holes, this can be removed with a pin, but be extremely careful not to damage the reeds.

If, despite your best efforts, reeds become damaged or blocked, don't attempt to dismantle the case and fix the problem yourself – you are far more likely to create further damage in doing so.

Some harmonicas can be repaired (particularly chromatic ones) or the retailer or manufacturer may replace a faulty instrument that has not been tampered with, but diatonic harmonicas are not expensive and you may just have to purchase a replacement.

When it comes to breaking in, soaking the harmonica can make it easier to play, as this softens the reeds, and can increase the volume for an experienced player, but it also shortens the harmonica's working life greatly and can lead to playing problems as the wood casing expands and shrinks. All manufacturers advise against soaking.

The best way to break in a new harmonica is to blow and draw through it gently for the first few days, and to avoid excessive volume or bending notes until it feels less stiff to play. Once it is broken in, remember to warm up gently, particularly in a cold room or outdoors.

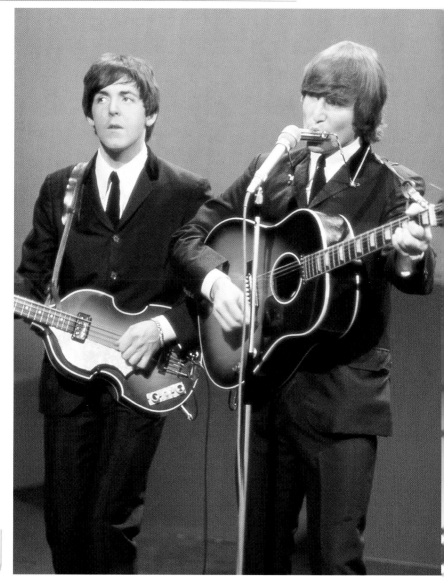

Chapter **2**

The basics of playing

'You really play that harmonica, don't you – I just blow and suck.'

John Lennon to Brian Jones of the Rolling Stones, 1963

John Lennon played the harmonica on most of the Beatles' early records.

Blowing and drawing

Many people imagine that getting a sound out of a harmonica is simply a matter of holding it in both hands and blowing and drawing as hard as possible. This is, however, far from the truth. As with any musical instrument, there are right ways and wrong ways; let's ignore the latter and concentrate on getting it right.

Holding the harmonica in one hand allows you to create muted and vibrato effects with the free hand (see Chapter 3). Hold the harmonica in your left hand as shown, with the lowest notes on the left.

Holding the harmonica

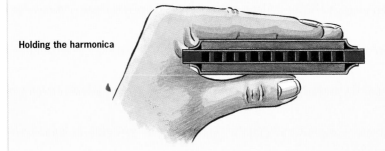

The next step is to work on blowing. Moisten your lips and part your teeth a little, then cover holes 1, 2 and 3 with your mouth and blow. Don't try to force the air through the reeds, but gently breathe from your chest in a relaxed way.

Keeping your mouth in the same position on the harmonica, draw on holes 1, 2 and 3. Again, try to inhale in as even and relaxed a way as possible. The temptation may be to snatch your breath inwards sharply or to be timid about drawing, but keep at it until you find yourself producing an even tone on both blowing and drawing.

Now stop and tap any saliva out of the harmonica (see page 18). If you are out of breath at this stage, you're probably trying too hard. Have another go, and concentrate on keeping your lips relaxed on the harmonica without being too tense.

Take another short break, and then practise the exercises shown below. When moving from holes 1, 2 and 3, keep the harmonica still and shift your head slightly so that your lips slide onto the next three holes. If this is difficult, remember to moisten your lips before playing and to keep them relaxed but definitely in position. To keep your breathing regular, beat time with your foot.

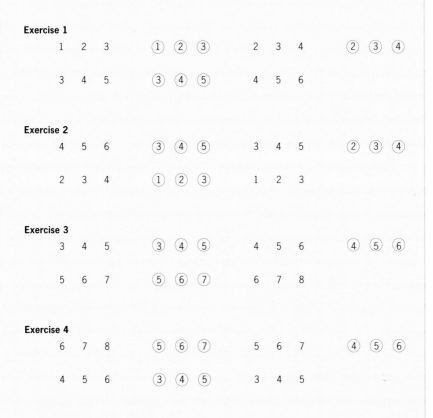

Exercise 1

1	2	3	①	②	③	2	3	4	②	③	④
3	4	5	③	④	⑤	4	5	6			

Exercise 2

4	5	6	③	④	⑤	3	4	5	②	③	④
2	3	4	①	②	③	1	2	3			

Exercise 3

3	4	5	③	④	⑤	4	5	6	④	⑤	⑥
5	6	7	⑤	⑥	⑦	6	7	8			

Exercise 4

6	7	8	⑤	⑥	⑦	5	6	7	④	⑤	⑥
4	5	6	③	④	⑤	3	4	5			

Chords and notes

Keeping your mouth open to cover two or three holes on the harmonica produces chords – groups of two or more notes. You can use chords to play tunes, with the melody on the top notes, but first practise moving all the way up and down the harmonica, again aiming for evenness of breath and movement.

Exercise 1

1 2 3　①②③　2 3 4　②③④　3 4 5　③④⑤　4 5 6　④⑤⑥

5 6 7　⑤⑥⑦　6 7 8　⑥⑦⑧　7 8 9　⑦⑧⑨　8 9 10　⑧⑨⑩

9 10 11　⑨⑩⑪　10 11 12　⑩⑪⑫　10 11 12　⑨⑩⑪　9 10 11　⑧⑨⑩

8 9 10　⑦⑧⑨　7 8 9　⑥⑦⑧　6 7 8　⑤⑥⑦　5 6 7　④⑤⑥

4 5 6　③④⑤　3 4 5　②③④　2 3 4　①②③　1 2 3

Using the top notes of these chords, you can play simple tunes, such as 'Frère Jacques' and 'Alouette'.

Frère Jacques

2 3 4　③④⑤　4 5 6　2 3 4　　2 3 4　③④⑤　4 5 6　2 3 4

4 5 6　④⑤⑥　5 6 7　4 5 6　④⑤⑥　5 6 7 | 5 6 7　⑤⑥⑦

5 6 7　④⑤⑥　4 5 6　2 3 4 | 5 6 7　⑤⑥⑦　5 6 7　④⑤⑥

4 5 6　2 3 4 | 2 3 4　③④⑤　2 3 4　2 3 4　③④⑤　2 3 4

Alouette

2 3 4   ③④⑤   4 5 6   4 5 6   ③④⑤   2 3 4   ③④⑤   4 5 6

2 3 4   1 2 3 | 2 3 4   ③④⑤   4 5 6   4 5 6   ③④⑤   2 3 4

③④⑤   4 5 6   2 3 4

However, very few tunes use only the chords that can be played on the diatonic harmonica. To progress further, you now need to be able to play single notes.

Blow a chord into holes 3, 4 and 5, and then pucker up your lips until only the middle of the three notes sounds – the shape you get should be like that used when whistling. Stop blowing, keep that position on your mouth and blow just the one note this time into hole 4, then draw breath in the same position. If you're getting more than one note, check that the shape of your lips is correct, and if necessary adjust the harmonica so that you can blow and draw single notes easily.

Try the tunes from the opposite page and other simple ones, this time concentrating solely on the melody.

Frère Jacques

5 ⑤ 6 5 5 ⑤ 6 5

6 ⑥ 7 6 ⑥ 7

7 ⑦ 7 ⑥ 6 5

7 ⑦ 7 ⑥ 6 5

5 ⑤/3 5 5 ⑤/3 5

In the last line, you can play either 5 or 3

Twinkle twinkle little star

5 5 7 7 ⑦⑦ 7

⑥⑥ 6 6 ⑤⑤ 5

7 7 ⑥⑥ 6 6 ⑤

7 7 ⑥⑥ 6 6 ⑤

5 5 7 7 ⑦⑦ 7

⑥⑥ 6 6 ⑤⑤ 5

Alouette

5 ⑤ 6 6 ⑤ 5 ⑤ 6 5 3

5 ⑤ 6 6 ⑤ 5 ⑤ 6 5

Beats and time

So far, the tunes that you have played are so well-known that their rhythms will have come to you as second nature. But what happens when you are faced with unfamiliar tunes? This is where a basic knowledge of reading music comes in handy.

Even a tune as simple as 'Frère Jacques' uses three different lengths of note and a system of counting the notes. If you imagine that each phrase of the song is one bar or measure, this can be counted in fours:

The three types of notes used are a quarter note, or crochet, equal to one beat, a half note, or minim, equal to two beats, and an eighth note, or quaver, equal to a half beat. In musical notation, they are written:

quarter note or crochet – **1 beat**

half note or minim – **2 beats**

eighth note or quaver – **½ beat**

Frère Jacques

1	2	3	4	1	2	3	4
Frè - re		Jac - ques,		Frè - re		Jac - ques,	

1	2	3	4	1	2	3	4
Dor - mez - vous?				Dor - mez - vous?			

1	2	3	4	1	2	3	4
Son- nez les ma- tin - es,				Son- nez les ma- tin - es,			

1	2	3	4	1	2	3	4
Ding	Dang	Dong,		Ding	Dang	Dong.	

Using these notes, 'Frère Jacques' looks like this:

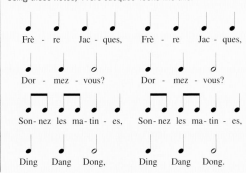

Frè - re   Jac - ques,   Frè - re   Jac - ques,

Dor - mez - vous?   Dor - mez - vous?

Son- nez les ma- tin - es,   Son- nez les ma- tin - es,

Ding   Dang   Dong,   Ding   Dang   Dong.

There are, of course, many other beats used, and these will be included in some of the examples later in this chapter. For now, a brief description of the main two will suffice:

○ whole note or semibreve – **4 beats**

♪ sixteenth note or semiquaver – **¼ beat**

As well as knowing the notation of the beats, you also need to know how a rest, when no notes are played, is shown:

▬ semibreve rest – **4 beats**

▬ minim rest – **2 beats**

𝄽 crochet rest – **1 beat**

𝄾 quaver rest – **½ beat**

𝄿 semiquaver rest – **¼ beat**

Many tunes use dotted notes, where the beat is extended:

𝅗𝅥· dotted half note or dotted minim – **3 beats**

♩· dotted quaver note or crochet – **1½ beats**

♪· dotted eigth note or quaver – **¾ beat**

The exercises on the next page are designed to help you familiarize yourself with reading notes and rests. Keep the beat with your foot while you are playing – and don't forget to tap saliva out of the harmonica at regular intervals!

Exercise 1

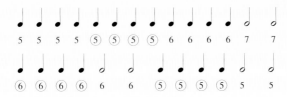

Exercise 2

Exercise 3

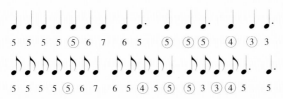

Exercise 4

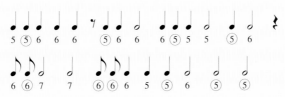

Reading music

Now that you know what the notes represent in terms of beats, it is a relatively easy matter to show how they link up with the notes you play on the harmonica. The music theory given here is designed to help you play tunes in the key of C major; there are many good books available to help you understand other keys and further your knowledge of theory.

The stave

Musical notation is written on staves, which consist of five parallel horizontal lines enclosing four spaces, all of which are used for notes:

Most music is written using one or two staves; the 12-hole diatonic harmonica in C uses the treble, or higher, clef, and music for bass harmonica, piano or guitar uses the bass, or lower clef:

The Treble Clef

The first two treble clef staves, shown below, correspond to the harmonica, while the third, bass clef stave is included as a comparison.

The Bass Clef

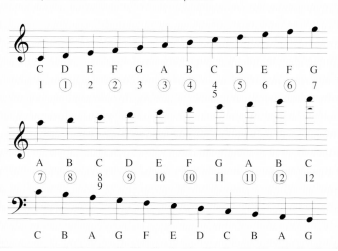

The example of notes on the treble clef on the previous page can be played, but a long stream of notes gives no idea of where to put the emphasis that gives life to a tune. To help you find the structure of a tune, the stave is divided up into bars or measures by vertical lines called bar lines. The first note after a bar line is emphasized. A double bar line denotes the end of a tune, while a 'dotted' double bar line at the beginning and end of a tune means that it is repeated.

Bar, double bar, and 'dotted' double bar lines

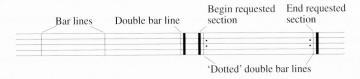

What goes in each bar is determined by the time signature. This is made up of two numbers, one on top of the other. The number on the top is for the number of beats in each measure, and the number on the bottom is for the type of note getting each beat. The latter relates to the notes shown on pages 26 and 27, and the most often used number is 4, which stands for four crotchets. It is theoretically possible to write music in almost any combination of time signatures – but not to play it! The signatures shown below are used in nearly all tunes in the fields of folk, country, blues and rock music.

Standard time signatures

$\frac{2}{4}$ Two crochets per bar; this is used for fast times, and it is faster than $\frac{4}{4}$

$\frac{3}{4}$ Three crochets per bar; otherwise known as 'waltz time', as all waltzes are in this signature

$\frac{4}{4}$ Four crochets per bar; the most used time signature in non-classical western musics, particularly for marching time and blues

$\frac{6}{8}$ Six quavers per bar; played with the emphasis on the first and fourth notes, this gives a jaunty, hornpipe feel

The key signature at the beginning of a tune tells you what notes should be played each time, unless instructed otherwise. These are related to the notes on a keyboard, with the white keys called the naturals, and the black ones the accidentals (sharps and flats). The key of C has no sharps and flats in its scale – the notes are C, D, E, F, G, A and B – so a piece of music that has no sharps and flats before the time signature will be in this key.

A chromatic harmonica can be used to play in all keys, but a diatonic harmonica plays only its own key, unless you play blues harmonica in the crossed harp method (see Chapter 3). If you want to play in other keys, you should buy diatonic harmonicas in those keys. The key signatures for diatonic harmonicas are given below.

Within a tune, a note may have a sharp – # – or flat – ♭ – sign next to it; this denotes that that note should be played sharp or flat within that bar, whatever the key signature.

Right: Often the simplest harmonica designs are the most comfortable to play and hold.

Scales and arpeggios

Practising scales is one of the best ways of learning how to find any single note on any instrument without having to think about it; on a harmonica, where you can't see what you're doing, it is no less than vital.

Start with a scale of C on the bottom octave:

Then practise the middle octave:

Put the two together, and then practise the top octave before adding it to the others.

Arpeggios are the four single notes that make up chords in a key; in the key of C, they are C, E, G and C. Play the arpeggios of the bottom octave as shown below, then add the middle and top octaves as before. This is a very good way of learning to move around the notes of the harmonica quickly and fluently.

Putting it all together

The musical theory in the previous pages may have seemed like hard work, getting in the way of what you really want to do – play the harmonica. However, once you start expanding your repertoire you will find it vital when you come to gathering new tunes to play; harmonica notation is only used in instruction books such as this, so you're on your own after that. In addition, being able to read and play a piece of music can lead to all sorts of unexpected delights and discoveries: you may find yourself faced with a tune without a title or that you've never heard of, and being able to interpret it is a very useful skill.

To test your knowledge, try playing this short tune, written without any harmonica notation:

Recognize it? It won't come round again, as you move onto tunes that incorporate all the theory and techniques you've learnt so far. As you go through the tunes, work on your interpretation of each one – it is all very well being able to play the right notes in the correct rhythm, but that is less than half of what makes an interesting musical performance. Try playing the tunes at different tempos – fast, slow and in-between – and experiment with adding chords to the single notes – some may fit, others not, but this process of exploration, once you are familiar with the written notes, adds enjoyment and proficiency to your playing.

London Bridge

Good Night, Ladies

Three Blind Mice

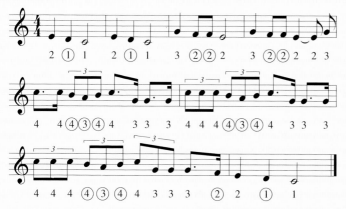

Oh, Suzanna

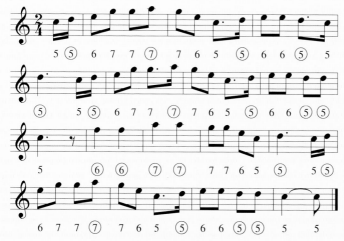

Good King Wenceslas

Amazing Grace

London's Burning

John Brown's Body

My Darling Clementine

Molly Malone

There's a Hole in my Bucket

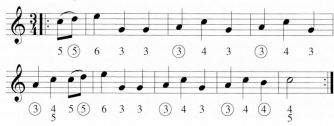

My Bonnie

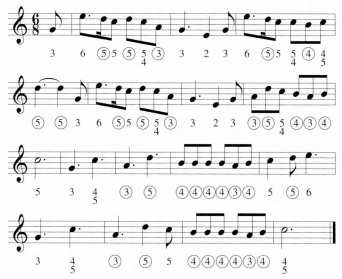

Camptown Races

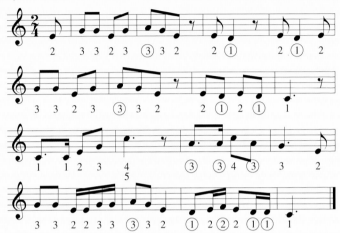

Jingle Bells

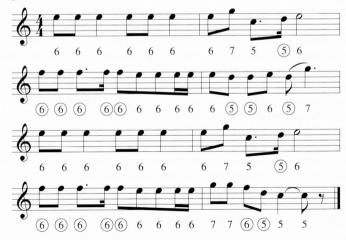

Au Clair de la Lune

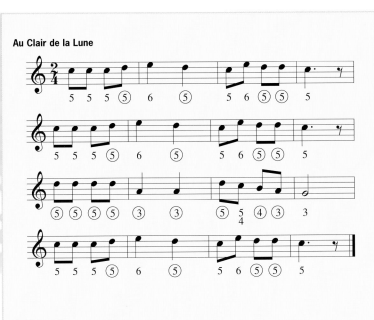

Auld Lang Syne

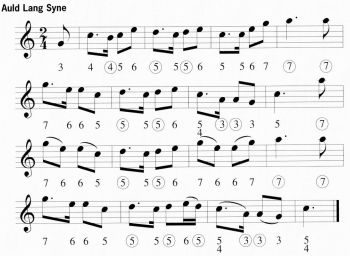

Chapter **3**

Advanced techniques and blues playing

'Sonny Boy worked his harmonica like a brass section, backward and inside out. He played it sticking out of his mouth like a cigar! He put the whole harp inside his mouth and played. . . .'

Levon Helm of The Band describing Sonny Boy Williamson in 1965

Sonny Boy Williamson's tough, virtuoso blues playing influenced a whole generation of harmonica players.

Tonguing, talking and vibrato

This chapter is about progressing from being a player of tunes on the harmonica to being a harmonica player. If you have worked at and mastered the basic tunes on pages 34–41, you may be wondering how to make them sound like your own interpretation and take them further – even if Sonny Boy Williamson's party tricks may be beyond your aspirations!

One of the first tricks of the trade is tonguing when you play. In fact, 'tonguing' describes two different techniques; the first of these involves making a chord shape with your mouth and then pushing your tongue forward so that it touches two out of the three holes on the harmonica. This technique is mainly used for getting clean single notes on a chromatic harmonica, and is hardly, if ever, used on a diatonic harmonica.

Tonguing on a diatonic harmonica is best learnt without the instrument at first. Whisper the sound 't' a few times and note how your tongue starts the sound at the roof of your mouth before dropping down. Now whisper 'tooo', with your breath coming from down in your diaphragm. Put the harmonica to your lips and whisper again, concentrating on making a definite start to each set of notes, then repeat the exercise while drawing. This gives a percussive effect that is very effective in giving emphasis to notes.

One of the most expressive effects that is unique to the harmonica is talking through it while playing. This is an integral part of good blues playing, and is very simple to learn. You can use any percussive-starting sound, such as 'tah-tah', 'teet-teet', 'doh-doh', 'dah-dah, 'toil-toil' or any combination of these and other sounds. Practise blowing and drawing these sound on chords at first, then add them to single notes and parts of tunes.

Vibrato is another marvellous effect, heard at its best on the diatonic harmonica. To achieve this, you need to create a sound chamber using your free hand. There are two common positions for this; experiment to find which suits you best, or make up your own chamber position.

Hands making chambers

While playing chords, rapidly move the free hand back and forth against the hand holding the harmonica; this opens and closes the sound chamber and creates a vibrato.

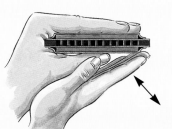 

Direction of free hand

Concentrate on getting the same amount of vibrato on both blown and drawn notes, and then practise varying vibrato speed on familiar tunes. As with all the techniques described in this chapter, don't be tempted to use vibrato all the time, otherwise everything will sound the same.

Playing blues harmonica

When the harmonica was invented and perfected over a century and a half ago, there was no such thing as blues music as we know it today. But the diatonic harmonica has become so associated with blues that it is reckoned that over half the harmonicas manufactured and sold are marketed as 'blues' models, some models even being made with lighter-weight reeds for easier bending techniques.

The influence of blues harmonica is everywhere – folk, jazz and country musicians use blues techniques to play types of music far removed from the traditional blues forms, and almost all rock harmonica is in direct descent from blues playing. Many would argue that blues gives the harmonica the chance to shine in a number of roles: as a chugging, gutsy rhythm instrument, as a wailing counterpoint to the human voice, and as a virtuoso solo instrument, capable of being played quietly and soulfully or being amplified to drown out a full band.

Why should this be the case? One of the main reasons is probably that the form of the blues is, for the most part, based around three chords: the tonic, subdominant and dominant. In any key, the tonic chord is based on the first note of the scale, the subdominant on the fourth and the dominant on the fifth, so in the key of C, the tonic chord is C, the subdominant F and the dominant G. The chart below gives the tonic, subdominant and dominant chords for the range of diatonic harmonicas.

Key of Harmonics	Tonic chord	Subdominant chord	Dominant chord
C	C	F	G
D	D	G	A
E	E	A	B
F	F	B♭	C
G	G	C	D
A	A	D	E
B♭	B♭	E♭	F

The traditional 12-bar blues is in 4/4 time and goes: 4 bars tonic, 2 bars subdominant, 2 bars tonic, 1 bar dominant, 1 bar subdominant and 2 bars tonic. So the chords in C would be:

chords for 12-bar in C

1 BAR											
C	C	C	C	F	F	C	C	G	F	C	C

There are literally dozens of variations on this progression, and minor chords are often used, but all these variants are based soundly on the 12-bar version. In the same way, every great blues player has found a style that is unique to him- or herself, however much it may owe to others: Sonny Terry, Little Walter and John Mayall are all classed together as 'blues harmonica players', but a quick listen shows that they all use the blues as a vehicle for their own personal musicianship and creativity.

The harmonica techniques and exercise in this chapter are intended to help you familiarize yourself with the blues form and be able to play some of the more common stock of blues patterns and variations. Once you have mastered them, listen to as many different players as possible and look out for what makes them unique and special. Sometimes this may be obvious – Captain Beefheart blended a virtuoso Delta blues harmonica technique with almost free-form jazz-rock to create an unmistakable sound – or it may be more subtle, but by absorbing and learning from the masters, you will become more adept.

Bending notes

Of all the blues techniques, bending is the most evocative, and at the same time the hardest to describe in words. Technically speaking, it is a way of lowering the pitch of a reed by drawing in air at a lower angle, thus bending the reed temporarily out of its normal position. Because of the construction of the harmonica (see page 14), you can't bend blown notes.

The easiest reeds to bend are the longest ones, those on mouth holes 1, 2, 3, 4, 5 and 6, and you should begin by working on these. It's a good idea to play in the harmonica first, so that the reeds are warmed up and will not be damaged permanently. Draw through hole 1 as usual, then pull your tongue down and back into your throat, drawing in your breath more strongly from deep in your diaphragm and slackening your jaw to allow your tongue to move down. You should hear the pitch of the note being lowered as you do this – a bend.

If nothing seems to happen, keep trying and, if necessary, use one of the higher holes, such as 3 or 4, for practice. Once you get a bend, start again on hole 1, drawing normally, bending the note, then drawing normally again; work your way up the holes to 5 and going back again. Take frequent breaks, to make sure that you don't hyperventilate, and don't be discouraged if you appear not to be making progress – any harmonica player will tell you that getting started on bending is hard work that takes time.

On a C harmonica, these are the notes that can be made by bending the pitch by a semitone:

Mouth hole	① ② ③ ④ ⑤ ⑥ ⑦ ⑧
Drawn note	D F A B D F A B
Bent note	C# E A♭ B♭ C# E A♭ B♭

Holes ⑨ – ⑫ duplicate holes ⑤ – ⑧, but are very difficult to bend

Of course, you don't have to use bending only for playing blues – using it subtly, you can play certain sharps and flats in conventional tunes, but approach this method with caution!

A technique often used in conjunction with bending notes is warbling, though it is equally effective used on its own. To get a warble, draw on one hole then, in the same breath, on the hole next to it (either higher or lower – it doesn't matter at this stage), then back to the first hole and then the second, still on the same draw. Build up speed, moving either the harmonica on your lips – the easier method – or your mouth on the harmonica. Next, try blowing a warble, and then practise drawing and blowing alternately. As you become more fluent at this, you can extend the warble over three notes or more; and then bend notes while warbling.

Straight harp blues

The term 'straight' or 'straight harp' blues refers to blues progressions that are played in the same key that the harmonica is tuned in; for a blues in C you would use a C harmonica, for one in D a D harmonica, and so on.

Although this might seem logical, in fact straight harp blues is very limited in comparison with crossed harp playing (*see* page 52), where the full range of bending notes – virtually impossible in straight harp – allows you to create exciting patterns and solos. However, straight harp should not be dismissed, because it is a good way to get used to playing the chordal structure of the main blues progressions; in addition, a great deal of folk and country music uses straight harp styles.

To go back to the chords on page 47, this simple exercise follows the standard 12-bar progression:

**12-bar
straight harp
in C**

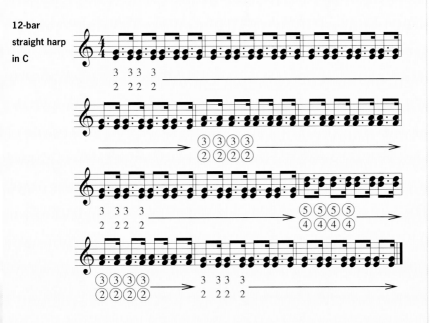

Taking this chordal structure as a base, now add a few variations of notes and timing to make the progression more interesting to play and hear:

12-bar variations

You can add rhythmic variations, such as playing the same pattern talking into the harmonica (see page 44): for instance, play the first four bars saying 'taah-ta-ta-taah', which immediately gives a dotted, dancing feel. And don't think that you have to play all the way through – rests bring dynamics and tension into the music.

The tunes on pages 58 and 59 are for practising straight harp blues styles; you will see that they do not follow the traditional 12-bar progression exactly, but they have all the elements of blues playing. When you play them, experiment with the tempo and add variations of your own, using tonguing, talking, vibrato and warbling (though not necessarily all at once). Try to make them sound bluesy or far removed from what you think of as the blues.

Crossed harp blues

When playing straight harp blues, you'll notice that it doesn't have the tension and excitement that you associate with blues harmonica. To achieve this, you have to play in crossed harp tunings. In these, you use a harmonica tuned to the subdominant key of the tune. To play crossed harp in C, you use a harmonica tuned to F. The chart below gives the crossed harp keys available from diatonic harmonicas:

Key of Harmonics	C	D	E	F	G	A	B♭
Crossed Harp Key	G	A	B	C	D	E	F

The C harmonica is used for blues tunes in G, so the musical notation for the exercises and tunes for crossed harp will be have the key signature for G:

Treble clef with G key signature

When playing straight harp, the chord of G, the dominant, was drawn; G is now the tonic chord, so you start the standard 12-bar progression by drawing for four bars. Don't try to draw too hard, or you'll run out of breath.

12-bar exercise in G

Now try varying this basic theme; you can also bend the drawn notes and use vibrato – if it sounds good, do it again and remember it, and if it doesn't, go back to the basics and try again.

The next step is to build up a pool of blues patterns and riffs that you can use to break up the rhythmic base. These have been written in harmonica notation, so that you can put your own emphasis and timing on them and use them in your own way.

As with the straight harp, listen out for different rhythms and breaks. Remember that with the blues, because the basic structures are relatively simple, it is the player's interpretation and inventiveness upon these structures that makes a blues tune exciting.

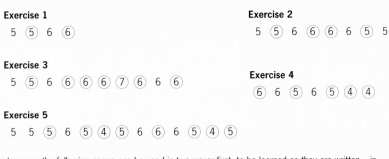

Exercise 1

5 (5) 6 (6)

Exercise 2

5 (5) 6 (6) (6) 6 (5) 5

Exercise 3

5 (5) 6 (6) (6) (6) (7) (6) 6 (6)

Exercise 4

(6) 6 (5) 6 (5) (4) (4)

Exercise 5

5 5 (5) 6 (5) (4) (5) 6 (6) 6 (5) (4) (5)

The tunes on the following pages can be used in two ways: first, to be learned as they are written – in standard notation, without the harmonica notation. This may seem daunting to begin with, but persevere; being able to sight-read music is one of the most useful tools in a musician's repertoire, and the familiarity of the majority of these tunes means that you will be able to tell whether or not you are playing the right notes.

The second purpose of the tunes is to bring in the techniques described in this chapter. Talking and vibrato can make all the difference when it comes to interpreting a tune, rather than just followng the notation – but use them sparingly, otherwise the result can sound like a parody of the real thing. In the same way, bending notes doesn't have to be confined to blues and blues-based tunes, and can liven up a well-known piece very effectively.

The next stage is to go and learn more tunes. You can do this from both sheet music and by ear; the latter is essential when learning blues riffs and tunes, as very few of these have been written down in any form of notation. Listen hard to recordings, talk to experienced players, practise – and have fun as you do. Good luck!

Silent Night

Swing Low, Sweet Chariot

Daisy Bell

Cannonball Blues

The Old Kentucky Home

Pack up your Troubles in your Old Kit Bag

Dixie Land

Early One Morning

Worried Man Blues

Careless Love

Frankie and Johnny

Old Joe Clark

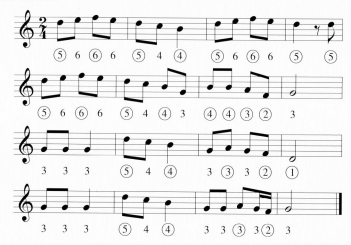

Corinna, Corinna

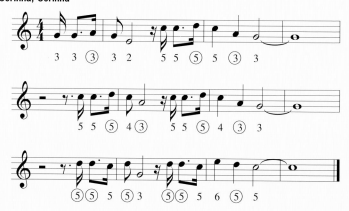

A few blues progression variations (*see* page 47) T = tonic, S = subdominant, D = dominant

1 | T | S | T | T | S | S | T | T | D | D | T | T ‖

2 | D | T | D | T | S | T | D | T | D | S | T | D ‖

3 | S | D | T | D | S | D | T | T | S | D | T | T ‖

Some basic blues rhythms

Players and influences

It would be impossible to even attempt to make a comprehensive list of great harmonica players – it would take up too much of the book, and the problem with trying to be all-inclusive is that someone's favourite slips through the net. So the names included here have been chosen because they have all used the harmonica adventurously and in perfect harmony with their chosen styles of music.

It has also proved very difficult to compile a discography, because in some cases the albums are out of print, or different companies have released the same record in different countries, or because re-releases may be of inferior quality. However, all these players are worth seeking out for their harmonica playing; even if the type of music doesn't appeal to you, listen to how they use the harmonica and enjoy all the sounds and emotions that can be coaxed from this little instrument!

Among the hundreds of blues harmonica players, a few names stand out head and shoulders above the rest, particularly as influences. Both Sonny Boy Williamsons were masters of rural harmonica, and Sonny Terry's country blues playing, particularly with Brownie McGee, has been carried on by such players as Tony 'Little Son' Glover and John Mayall. The urban, electric blues style is typified by Little Walter, with James Cotton, Junior Wells and Howlin' Wolf providing different slants. The blues revival of the 1960s gave prominence to players such as Paul Butterfield, Bob Hite of Canned Heat and Lee Brilleaux of Dr Feelgood. Their influence was carried into the pop-rock field by Brian Jones of the Rolling Stones, Paul Jones of the Blues Band, Captain Beefheart and John Lennon, among many others.

Country and folk harmonica became popularized in rock by Bob Dylan, of course, as well as Neil Young, Donovan and Bruce Springsteen. Charlie McCoy, Chaim Tannenbaum, Woody Guthrie and Harmonica Frank Floyd are associated with country harmonica, while Willie Atkinson, Rory McLeod, Chris Taylor, Martin Brinsford and Brendan Power are among the foremost folk harmonica players. Jazz is primarily associated with the chromatic harmonica; Larry Adler, Tommy Reilly, Toots Thielmans and Max Geldray are among the big names, while Stevie Wonder has developed a jazz/funk hybrid all of his own.

Neil Young's plaintive country harmonica is instantly recognizable.

Index of Tunes